YOU'VE GOAT THIS

YOU'VE GOAT THIS

WISDOM TO GET YOU THROUGH THE GOOD, THE BAAAD, AND EVERYTHING IN BETWEEN

APOLLO
PUBLISHERS

You've Goat This: Wisdom to Get You Through
the Good, the Baaad, and Everything in Between
Copyright © 2020 by Apollo Publishers
Interior images © 2020 by Goats Gone Grazing Acres

Apollo Publishers books may be purchased for educational, business, or sales promotional use. Special editions may be made available upon request. For details, contact Apollo Publishers at info@apollopublishers.com.

Visit our website at www.apollopublishers.com.

Published in compliance with California's Proposition 65.

Library of Congress Cataloging-in-Publication Data is available on file.

Print ISBN: 978-1-948062-50-3
Ebook ISBN: 978-1-948062-51-0

Printed in the United States of America.

Contents

EWE CAN DO IT! 7

THINKING OUTSIDE THE BARN 45

THE UDDER HALF 79

HANDLING YOUR HERD 93

THE GOAT LIFE 129

AGING GRAZEFULLY 159

GOAT VIBES 177

EWE DO EWE 203

ABOUT THE GOATS 240

1

EWE CAN DO IT!

It's the choice
you have to wake
up everyday and say,
"There's no reason
today can't be the
best day of my life."

———

BLAKE LIVELY

If you want
the best
things in life,
you have to
earn them
for yourself.

———

JAYNE MANSFIELD

The secret to getting ahead is getting started.

MARK TWAIN

Success usually comes to those who are too busy to look for it.

HENRY DAVID THOREAU

One may walk over the highest mountain one step at a time.

BARBARA WALTERS

If you're walking down the right path and you're willing to keep walking, eventually you'll make progress.

———

BARACK OBAMA

A wise girl knows
her limits. A smart girl
knows she has none.

—————

MARILYN MONROE

Make more than the guys you thought you wanted to be with.

Stay hungry,
stay foolish.

———

STEVE JOBS

It's always fun to defy expectations.

MARTIN SHORT

It's not the size of the dog in the fight, it's the size of the fight in the dog.

MARK TWAIN

Cupcakes are muffins that believed in miracles.

UNKNOWN

I'm trying to do better
than good enough.

DRAKE

Be so good they can't ignore you.

——

STEVE MARTIN

COURAGE • 23

Believe you can and you're halfway there.

———

THEODORE ROOSEVELT

Nothing is impossible to a determined woman.

LOUISA MAY ALCOTT

To hell with circumstances;
I create opportunities.

———

They will try to close the
door on you. Just open it.

———

DJ KHALED

Expect problems
and eat them for breakfast.

ALFRED A. MONTAPERT

I pity the fool
who just gives up.

———

MR. T

Only one thing is ever guaranteed, that is that you will definitely not achieve the goal if you don't take the shot.

WAYNE GRETZKY

If you're offered a seat on a rocket ship, don't ask what seat! Just get on.

———

SHERYL SANDBERG

I don't want easy.
Easy doesn't make you grow.
Easy doesn't make you think.

———

MADONNA

You have to look through rain to see the rainbow.

UNKNOWN

Life is like riding a bicycle. To keep your balance you must keep moving.

ALBERT EINSTEIN

If they can make penicillin out of moldy bread, they can sure make something out of you.

———

MUHAMMAD ALI

Show me a person who has never made a mistake, and I'll show you a person who has never achieved much.

JOAN COLLINS

Rock bottom became the solid foundation on which I built my life.

— J. K. ROWLING

Failure is the condiment that gives success its flavor.

———

TRUMAN CAPOTE

A diamond is merely a lump of coal that did well under pressure.

———

UNKNOWN

Everything will be okay in the end. If it's not okay, it's not the end.

JOHN LENNON

I've failed over and over again in my life. That is why I succeed.

MICHAEL JORDAN

2

THINKING
OUTSIDE
THE BARN

I knew that with a mouth like mine, I just had to be a star or something.

BARBRA STREISAND

I am my own muse.
I am the subject I know best.
The subject I want
to know better.

FRIDA KAHLO

If I'm going to sing
like somebody else, then
I don't need to sing at all.

—

BILLIE HOLIDAY

You're only given a little spark of madness. You mustn't lose it.

ROBIN WILLIAMS

It's hard to be funny when you have to be clean.

———

MAE WEST

I don't do drugs.
I am drugs.

———

SALVADOR DALÍ

Imperfection is beauty, madness is genius, and it's better to be absolutely ridiculous than absolutely boring.

MARILYN MONROE

I'm not trying to be sexy.
It's just my way of expressing
myself when I move around.

ELVIS PRESLEY

If you're trying too hard
to be the girl next door,
you're not going to be.

———

TAYLOR SWIFT

You have to go on and be crazy.
Craziness is like heaven.

———

JIMI HENDRIX

I won't be a rock star.
I will be a legend.

FREDDIE MERCURY

Without leaps of imagination, or dreaming, we lose the excitement of possibility. Dreaming, after all, is a form of planning.

GLORIA STEINEM

Just think what a dull world it would be if everyone was sensible.

LUCY MAUD MONTGOMERY

To succeed in life you need three things: a wishbone, a backbone, and a funny bone.

———

REBA MCENTIRE

Laughter is timeless, imagination has no age, and dreams are forever.

WALT DISNEY

It will never rain roses: when we want to have more roses, we must plant more roses.

—

GEORGE ELIOT

It is better to light a candle than to curse the darkness.

ELEANOR ROOSEVELT

Imagination is the true magic carpet.

NORMAN VINCENT
PEALE

If you obey all the rules,
you miss all the fun.

——

KATHARINE HEPBURN

Do what you love and you will be badass.

TERRY CREWS

There's power in looking silly and not caring that you do.

AMY POEHLER

I have to be creative
to be happy.

GWEN STEFANI

I'm afraid of nothing
except being bored.

GRETA GARBO

Failure is unimportant.
It takes courage to make
a fool of yourself.

CHARLIE CHAPLIN

I have a theory that the truth is never told during nine-to-five hours.

———

I've gone seventy-nine hours without sleep, creating.

———

Every stumble is not a fall. And every fall does not mean failure.

OPRAH WINFREY

You have to stop crying,
and you have to go kick some ass.

———

LADY GAGA

Just try new things. Don't be afraid. Step out of your comfort zone and soar, alright?

MICHELLE OBAMA

3

THE UDDER
HALF

I'm not what you might call sexy, but I'm romantic.

BETTY WHITE

Sex appeal is 50 percent
what you've got and 50 percent
what people think you've got.

SOPHIA LOREN

Save a boyfriend for a rainy day—and another in case it doesn't rain.

MAE WEST

I'm a big proponent
of all love winning and
love just being fab.

JONATHAN VAN NESS

You can't give your heart
to a wild thing.

———

TRUMAN CAPOTE

The best thing to
hold onto in life
is each other.

AUDREY
HEPBURN

**Love is the flower
you've got to let grow.**

—

JOHN LENNON

Honesty is the
key to a relationship.
If you can fake that, you're in.

———

RICHARD JENI

Of course I am not worried about intimidating men. The type of man who will be intimidated by me is exactly the type of man I have no interest in.

CHIMAMANDA NGOZI ADICHIE

I've always said to my men friends, if you really care for me darling, you will give me territory. Give me land, give me land.

EARTHA KITT

My weaknesses have always been food and men—in that order.

4

HANDLING
YOUR HERD

I am tough,
but deep inside
my toughness, I like
to let people know
I'm an old-fashioned
mama's boy.

MR. T

**Families are like fudge.
Mostly sweet with a few nuts.**

———

UNKNOWN

Because of their size, parents may be difficult to discipline properly.

P. J. O'ROURKE

Family means no one gets left behind or forgotten.

DAVID OGDEN STIERS

**A happy family
is but an earlier heaven.**

———

GEORGE BERNARD SHAW

The best place to cry is on a mother's arms.

JODI PICOULT

It is not flesh and blood,
but heart which makes
us fathers and sons.

———

FRIEDRICH VON SCHILLER

I say if you love
something, set it in a
small cage and pester
and smother it with
love until it either loves
you back or dies.

—

MINDY KALING

Anyone who tells you that fatherhood is the greatest thing that can happen to you, they are understating it.

———

MIKE MYERS

A mother is not a person to lean on, but a person to make leaning unnecessary.

DOROTHY CANFIELD FISHER

A brother is a friend given by nature.

———

JEAN-BAPTISTE LEGOUVÉ

Sisters are different flowers
from the same garden.

Tis the privilege
of a friendship
to talk nonsense,
and to have
her nonsense
respected.

_____

CHARLES LAMB

It's one of the blessings of old friends that you can afford to be stupid with them.

RALPH WALDO EMERSON

My idea of heaven is a great big baked potato and someone to share it with.

OPRAH WINFREY

Friendship is born at that moment when one person says to another, "What, you too? I thought I was the only one."

C. S. LEWIS

The love that comes from friendship is the underlying facet of a happy life.

——

We don't have to do
all of it alone. We were
never meant to.

———

BRENÉ BROWN

You know when I feel inwardly beautiful? When I am with my girlfriends and we are having a "goddess circle."

———

JENNIFER ANISTON

I'm not great
at small talk.

___

COURTENEY COX

When someone is cruel or acts like a bully, you don't stoop to their level. No, our motto is, when they go low, we go high.

———

MICHELLE OBAMA

I like long walks.
Especially if they are taken
by people who annoy me.

——————

FRED ALLEN

Be nice to nerds. Chances are you'll end up working for one.

BILL GATES

You can disagree without being disagreeable.

———

RUTH BADER GINSBURG

Deep breaths are very helpful at shallow parties.

BARBARA WALTERS

There's a thin line between to laugh with and to laugh at.

—

RICHARD PRYOR

Gossip is poison.

GISELE BÜNDCHEN

All you have to do to be my friend is like me.

TAYLOR SWIFT

**People with no humor,
they're outta my life.**

———

PATTI LABELLE

You make yourself broad. You make yourself appealing. "Hey y'all, I'm cool with everybody." That's my message.

———

KEVIN HART

5

THE
GOAT LIFE

It's important to remember that you're born naked and the rest is drag.

RUPAUL

If you're presenting yourself with confidence, you can pretty much pull off anything.

KATY PERRY

You're only as good as your last haircut.

———

FRAN LEBOWITZ

Style—all who have it share
one thing: originality.

_____

DIANA VREELAND

Christmas sweaters are only acceptable as a cry for help.

——————

ANDY BOROWITZ

My mother was right: when you've got nothing left, all you can do is get into silk underwear and start reading Proust.

JANE BIRKIN

You can pay for school but you can't buy class.

JAY Z

I like simple things.
Elastic waists, so I can eat.

————

BARBRA STREISAND

OUR HAPPY PLACE

It's always nice to make an effort when you get photographed.

——

RITA ORA

The only rule is don't be boring and dress cute wherever you go. Life is too short to blend in.

———

PARIS HILTON

Everything
you see
I owe to
spaghetti.

————

SOPHIA LOREN

All of the things I really like to do are either immoral, illegal, or fattening.

ALEXANDER WOOLLCOTT

I don't think
any day is
worth living
without thinking
about what
you're going
to eat next at
all times.

————

NORA EPHRON

Health food
may be good for
the conscience,
but Oreos
taste a hell of
a lot better.

ROBERT REDFORD

Cultivate your curves—they may be dangerous but they won't be avoided.

MAE WEST

The second day of a diet
is always easier than the first.
By the second day, you're off it.

———

JACKIE GLEASON

The only time to eat diet food is while you're waiting for the steak to cook.

JULIA CHILD

Winning isn't always championships.

————

MICHAEL JORDAN

Sleeping is a luxury.

VERA WANG

Me: unbothered, moisturized, in my lane, well-hydrated, flourishing.

CARDI B

No phone, a movie,
a glass of wine, and
some salad. Perfect!

KATE MOSS

I don't exercise.
If God had wanted me
to bend over, he would
have put diamonds
on the floor.

JOAN RIVERS

I promote
a healthy lifestyle.

———

KIM KARDASHIAN

Nothing burns more calories than dancing in five-inch heels.

————

ARIANA GRANDE

6

AGING
GRAZEFULLY

I don't feel old.
I don't feel anything until noon.
Then it's time for my nap.

———

BOB HOPE

The secret to staying young is to live honestly, eat slowly, and lie about your age.

———

LUCILLE BALL

I guess I don't so much mind being old as I mind being fat and old.

BENJAMIN FRANKLIN

We don't stop
playing because
we grow old;
we grow old
because we
stop playing.

GEORGE
BERNARD SHAW

Age is of no importance
unless you're a cheese.

BILLIE BURKE

I won't quit to become someone's old lady.

JANIS JOPLIN

Keep smiling, it takes ten years off.

———

UNKNOWN

AGE • 167

Old age is like everything
else. To make a success of it,
you've got to start young.

———

THEODORE ROOSEVELT

Wrinkles merely mark where smiles have been.

MARK TWAIN

I'm kind of comfortable with getting older because it is better than the other option, which is being dead.

GEORGE CLOONEY

If a song was
ever good, it's still good.

———

WILLIE NELSON

AGE · 171

I do the
New York Times
crossword puzzle
every morning to
keep the old gray
matter ticking.

———

CAROL BURNETT

I love my age.
Old enough to know better.
Young enough not to care.
Experienced enough
to do it right.

———

ANGELA BASSETT

When I'm in my fifties, I kind of think I'll want to be in a garden.

TAYLOR SWIFT

7

GOAT VIBES

I just want one day off
when I can go swimming
and eat ice cream and
look at rainbows.

MARIAH CAREY

I'm not a Twitterer. I'm not a twerker. I'm not a Facebooker. I'm not nothing. I'm old school.

MICHAEL JORDAN

Give me two hours a day of activity and I'll take the other twenty-two in dreams.

—

SALVADOR

DALÍ

When you play,
play hard; when
you work, don't
play at all.

———

THEODORE ROOSEVELT

I'm tired of hearing about money, money, money, money, money. I just want to play the game, drink Pepsi, wear Reebok.

———

SHAQUILLE O'NEAL

There is no such thing
in anyone's life as an
unimportant day.

———

ALEXANDER WOOLLCOTT

Adventure is not without man; it is within.

GEORGE ELIOT

BEWARE

OF

GOAT

I take my dog Tinkerbell seriously. I take my job seriously. But I don't take myself all that seriously.

PARIS HILTON

I've chosen to treat my life more like a party than something to stress about.

———

MARTIN SHORT

In real life,
I assure you,
there is no such
thing as algebra.

FRAN LEBOWITZ

You only live once, but if you do it right, once is enough.

MAE WEST

I'm an emotional gangster. I cry once every month.

CARDI B

Excuse me while I kiss the sky.

———

JIMI HENDRIX

Chaos is
a friend of mine.

———

BOB DYLAN

**One's destination
is never a place, but
a new way of seeing things.**

———

HENRY MILLER

The biggest adventure
you can take is to live
the life of your dreams.

OPRAH WINFREY

An early morning walk is a blessing for the whole day.

HENRY DAVID THOREAU

The clearest way into
the Universe is through
a forest wilderness.

JOHN MUIR

I am not
afraid of
storms, for
I am learning
how to sail
my ship.

_____

LOUISA MAY ALCOTT

Valor is stability, not of arms and legs, but of courage and the soul.

MICHEL DE MONTAIGNE

I'm a work in progress.

———

BARBRA STREISAND

I embrace mistakes.
They make you who you are.

———

BEYONCÉ

8

EWE
DO EWE

Don't worry about a thing, every little thing is gonna be alright.

——

BOB MARLEY

Attitude is a little thing that makes a big difference.

—————

WINSTON CHURCHILL

If you don't like something, change it. If you can't change it, change your attitude.

MAYA ANGELOU

———

I'll tell you what
freedom is to me: no fear.

——————

NINA SIMONE

I think you can be defiant and rebellious and still be strong and positive.

MADONNA

All serious daring starts from within.

———

EUDORA WELTY

Always be a first-rate version
of yourself, instead of a second-
rate version of somebody else.

———

JUDY GARLAND

You change the world
by being yourself.

———

YOKO ONO

Find out who you are
and do it on purpose.

————

DOLLY PARTON

Keep your face to
the sunshine and you
cannot see a shadow.

———

You are imperfect, you are wired for struggle, but you are worthy of love and belonging.

BRENÉ BROWN

When you ain't got no money,
you gotta get an attitude.

RICHARD PRYOR

The one thing that can solve most of our problems is dancing.

JAMES BROWN

Find your light; they can't love you if they can't see you.

—

BETTE MIDLER

Don't pay attention to what they write about you. Just measure it in inches.

———

ANDY WARHOL

Follow your
inner moonlight;
don't hide the madness.

———

ALLEN GINSBERG

You can be very wild and still be very wise.

YOKO ONO

If you haven't cried,
your eyes can't
be beautiful.

———

SOPHIA LOREN

I'm always making a comeback but nobody ever tells me where I've been.

BILLIE HOLIDAY

**What makes you different
or weird, that's your strength.**

———

MERYL STREEP

Joy is what happens to us when we allow ourselves to recognize how good things really are.

———

MARIANNE WILLIAMSON

Friendship with one's self is all important, because without it one cannot be friends with anyone else in the world.

———

ELEANOR ROOSEVELT

I knew that I was a winner back in the late sixties. I knew I was destined for great things. People will say that kind of thinking is totally immodest. I agree. Modesty is not a word that applies to me in any way—I hope it never will.

ARNOLD SCHWARZENEGGER

My only fault is that I don't realize how great I really am.

_____

MUHAMMAD ALI

Confidence
is sexy.

———

I am not a has-been.
I am a will-be.

——

LAUREN BACALL

It's hard to be a diamond in a rhinestone world.

DOLLY PARTON

Even the tiniest of flowers can have the toughest roots.

_____

SHANNON MULLEN

The minute you learn
to love yourself, you won't
want to be anyone else.

———

RIHANNA

Am I good
enough?
Yes, I am.

———

Be yourself;
everyone else is
already taken.

—————

OSCAR WILDE

If you're always trying to be normal, you'll never know how amazing you can be.

—

MAYA ANGELOU

About the Goats

The goats in this book live on Goats Gone Grazing Acres, a small, working goat farm run by two city folks gone rogue, Jessi and Josh Pottebaum. The farm opened operations in 2009 with two goats, Suzie Q and Sophie Lou. Since then, the herd has grown in size from two to fifty-four goats, and their photos have gone viral on Instagram (@goats_gone_grazing_acres), reaching more than thirty-eight thousand followers, and been featured in Buzzfeed and Mashable. Goats Gone Grazing Acres is proud to have healthy, well-cared for goats and to promote the love of animals, including for its chickens, pack of guardian dogs, and its cow, Fred Asteer. The farm is located in western Kentucky.